THANK YOU!

Before you get started we would like to say a massive thank you for your purchase!
We hope that you like it.

Your REVIEW means a lot to us!

We would be so grateful if you could spare a few minutes of your time to leave us a review on Amazon.
We are a 2 person team trying to compete with huge brands and reviews help us get seen.

Let's be friends?

If you would like to stay connected, share comments or suggestions, then we invite you to follow / message / tag us:
- on Amazon
- on Instagram: @Adjustandachieve
- by email: Adjustandachieve@gmail.com

Printed in Poland
by Amazon Fulfillment
Poland Sp. z o.o., Wrocław
23 April 2022

b24a9fcb-9f77-4b90-9b33-52205a522062R01